9 Killer Mistakes Men Make In Divorce

Is Divorce Advice For Men
Different Than For Women? Yes!
Here's A Common Sense Guide For
A Better Life After Divorce.

E. James Marsh

Copyright 2011

Smashwords Edition

Preface

Nine is considered a good number in Chinese culture because it sounds the same as the word "long-lasting." Nine is strongly associated with the Chinese dragon, a symbol of magic and power.

9 Publishing Company

P.O. Box 14808

Portland, Oregon 97293

Table of Contents

Introduction

It's been said that the three toughest things to deal with in life are death, divorce and the loss of a job. I've lived long enough to tell you I won't argue with any of that--I've experienced all three.

But it took my own divorce and those of many friends to see that some light needed to be shed on divorce and a man's life. While there are hundreds of books out there by noted lawyers, psychologists, educators, gurus, I found few offer some simple golden nuggets to help you get through this painful period.

As liberated as this world is now, men still get screwed more often than women. Our justice system is way behind the times. And divorcing wives (and their attorneys) use this well-known fact to their advantage time and again. Whether it involves children, division of assets or anything in between, divorcing husbands are almost always on the short end of the stick.

So just what is a guy to do?

You need some very good advice. I'm hopeful this guide is a step in the right direction.

In it, you will find some proven (and personally tested) thoughts simple yet sometimes so easy to ignore because of the pain and drama you're dealing with. But I found that by following these 9 gems I was able to get through with my divorce with integrity and health still intact.

It is my genuine belief that they can do the same for you if you are dealing with a painful divorce, and want to enjoy a better life in the future.

Killer Mistake #1: Not Seeing an Attorney Right Away

When a wife tells a husband she wants a divorce, he is usually shell-shocked. The idea of this woman whose promise was to "love you in good times and in bad" ditching you doesn't sit well at all. You're thinking, well counseling will fix this, or this is just a bad mood of hers, or period-related. In other words, you rationalize that this is just a small blip on the radar screen of life, and yes "it, too, shall pass."

So you go on about your business pleading, begging or subjecting yourself to her demands.

But I've got news for you: once most women have made up their minds to separate and divorce you, it's pretty much a done deal. Why? Well it's because they've been going over this in their minds for a lot longer than you realize…weeks, months and sometimes even years. They could be in an affair. Maybe they're hiding assets from you. (I'm familiar with both.)

Whatever the case, it's critical you see an attorney right away. Find out where you stand on child custody issues, division of assets, spousal support or who lives in the marital home.

This consultation with an attorney should not be put off regardless of how optimistic you are about your marriage. The advice you will receive will help put your mind at ease because you will know where you stand.

How do you find the right attorney?

First of all, you should inquire of family and close friends. Ask them about attorneys they know or have heard about. If you don't have that option, check with your local bar association. It is the membership group of lawyers and responsible for the regulation of the legal profession in their jurisdiction. They will be able to give you names of the attorneys who specialize in "domestic relations."

Do your due diligence on the web. Many clients provide reviews of their attorneys. Go to online forums and see what they say. Just go ahead and "google" your "county" and "bar association."

Remember: "fear of the unknown" is a terrible place to be. You want to know what your options are, how your assets could be divided, how the court will treat you in regard to child custody.

Do not put off this initial contact with an attorney. Even if your marriage does survive, it is money well spent.

Killer Mistake #2: Not Getting To the Gym

Exercise can single-handedly be your life-saver during a divorce. Let's face it: your wife serves you with papers or you found out she's having an affair. And you're stunned or saddened or angry…most likely all of the above.

Then you start finding yourself paralyzed about what to do. "I need to call an attorney" or "What am I going to do?" or "I need to get laid!" are all common thoughts racing through your head. But not one of them can have the immediate healing effect of getting some exercise.

Taking care of your cardio-vascular system keeps a lot of bad stuff away. Endorphins released during an extended cardio exercise will give you a temporary high and take away your visits to "negative town." Whatever the work out, you need to do it every day.

In the first month of separation during my divorce, I couldn't drag my butt to the gym. I was too depressed. I lost 30 pounds in 3 weeks…not the healthiest way to manage your weight. Finally my brother said "get thou to the gym now."

I did and I've been going religiously ever since, at least 4-5 times a week. You will not only begin to feel better about yourself, but you will start to look better. You will drop pounds, reactivate muscles and sleep better.

If you don't know where to start, think about getting a personal trainer to get you on the right program. In many cases, you get a free consultation with one after joining a fitness facility.

Remember: with regular exercise you are not only rebuilding your body. You are ramping up your self-confidence. And as you already know, nothing is more attractive to the opposite sex than confidence.

Killer Mistake #3: Not Seeing a Therapist

After I initially separated from my ex-wife, I implored her to go into couples counseling with me. I truly thought there was hope of repairing the marriage even after her affair.

But when she told me she believed "counseling was only for us to feel better about the divorce," a light bulb went on and I got a "clarity" moment. I was done, finished…no more wasted time on "us" or "her." Instead, it became all about me.

I started seeing my therapist weekly. Every Wednesday we discussed whatever was on my mind…and as you might have guessed, the topic of discussion during my 55-minute sessions have almost always included relationship issues.

It has been the best investment for me mentally and emotionally. I throw out whatever's on my mind and we turn it inside out and try to make some sense of it. No judging, no lashing out, no manipulating as my ex-wife was so good at doing. We just made plain and simple observations about why "I'm feeling the way I'm feeling."

What's truly amazing about individual therapy is that you feel incredibly safe discussing some of your worst fears, thoughts and ideas. You'll learn why they have shaped and molded you, and what part they play in any of your relationships…with your children, family and friends.

Unfortunately, too many men wait to get into personal counseling. They become paralyzed in their thinking, choosing to wallow in their grief, while becoming lethargic. And while that is perfectly understandable, these actions do nothing to help you to move on and heal from this major life passage.

As in choosing an attorney, you'll find a good competent therapist through your friends and family. In fact, I found my therapist whom I've been seeing over the past 20 years on and off through my cousin.

What's more, there are plenty of local support groups as well as online groups with people experiencing similar thoughts and feelings as you. (You'll find a few listed in the resources guide at the back of this guide.) Your church can also help you find a good resource.

Don't put off getting help. You will reap the mental and emotional benefits quickly.

Killer Mistake #4: Not Taking Care of Finances

It is difficult to deal with everyday life when you're going through a divorce. You feel lousy both physically and emotionally. But in spite of that, you need to take care of your financial situation as soon as possible.

After meeting with your attorney, you need to sort out all the assets and get a general feeling of who is going to get what. This includes bank accounts, retirement accounts, real estate investments, life insurance, stock plans and the martial home.

There are many things you can do to protect yourself. If you've yet to be served with divorce papers from your soon-to-be-ex, you can change your will so that half of your estate goes to your family (children, siblings, parents) if you die before the divorce decree gets signed. Otherwise, your entire estate could go to the woman you're divorcing (check your state's laws or consult with an attorney). You can also change the beneficiary of your life insurance plan as well.

One other important thing to do before you're served is to close out joint banking and credit card accounts. And open up new ones in your name only. I made the mistake of not knowing my ex-wife was on one of my checking accounts and she took $1,300 out of it before I knew. I'll never get it back.

Don't forget about your health insurance either. If you're on her plan, she has to keep you there until the divorce decree is signed, or vice-versa. But if you're on her plan, you need to start shopping so you're ready when everything's done. It is a terrible idea to be without major medical coverage, at the least.

Also figure out how much you're going to need to live on. Stay on a budget if you've moved out and keep track of your expenses. In many cases, men now have legal rights to spousal support if your ex-wife-to-be earned more than you.

If you do not have a current document of the net wealth you and your ex have accumulated, you need to get that in order too. Most attorneys or your CPA can provide you with a simple file to input that information. It is basically assets minus liabilities to get a good idea of how much your estate is valued. I've included a resource at the back of this guide.

Killer Mistake #5: Not Telling Your Family and Friends Right Away

It is quite understandable that you don't want to tell your close family and friends about your separation and pending divorce. Most men have incredible pride. So if your wife cheated on you or left you because you weren't "successful" in her eyes, you feel some shame. And you're not likely to want to blast your situation out to your inner circle.

But that could be a big mistake. The classic male pattern is to internalize everything…and your health pays a huge price. Heart problems, strokes, ulcers are all well-known by-products of keeping things to yourself.

When you tell your family and close friends, you feel awkward at first…but afterwards you feel a sense of relief as if a giant boulder has been lifted off your shoulders. In today's world, just about everyone knows someone who has been through a bad divorce (Is there such a thing as a good divorce?) If they are true friends, they will not judge you. You will only receive unconditional love and moral support.

Personally, I remember telling my own mom and dad. They had been married over 40 years at the time. My mom in particular had strong beliefs about divorce. But she told me everything would be okay...said to go ahead and cry if I felt like it. And I had nothing but full and unconditional love and support from both of them.

Telling your work associates is a bit trickier. You want to be careful who you inform about your pending divorce. Some people might immediately think your job performance may be affected. (In all likelihood, it will.)

Best idea would be to just tell your immediate boss in confidence. Let him or her know you are working through it and don't plan the divorce to be a distraction to your daily duties on the job. They might even encourage you to take some time off, if your company offers sick leave or you've accrued vacation time. It's a good idea if you can make it work financially.

If there are children from your marriage, you and your soon-to-be-ex need to tell them about the divorce. The best idea on how to discuss that would be to seek advice from your therapist. Even if the sight of your ex makes you sick to your stomach, you need to try and be united in the message you tell your children.

During my divorce, my sons were in their young 20s and I felt they needed to know their mom was having an affair. I told them in as non-judgmental way as possible. The funny thing is, they already knew about it as did my stepsons.

Killer Mistake #6: Not Getting Proper Nutrition

When you're first dealing with a divorce, it is difficult to eat anything. You feel weak, nauseated and chronically fatigued. At least that was the case for me.

I had no problem drinking a glass or two of wine to provide a bit of temporary relief. In fact, that is a big problem with men. We find it all too easy to pound down a few beers…liquor or wine. But self-medicating isn't the answer.

And then when you feel like eating, it's usually junk food because you don't have the energy to cook anything for yourself. Burgers, burritos and pizza are laden with fat and cholesterol. The problem is that such a lousy diet saps your energy even further.

That's why you need to work very hard at eating good things. You've heard the litany before but here they are again for a reminder, this from the Mayo Clinic:

- ✓ Eat more fruits, vegetables and whole grains
- ✓ Reduce intake of animal foods

- ✓ Substitute healthy plant fats in place of saturated and trans fats
- ✓ Limit sweets and salt
- ✓ Control portion sizes and the total number of calories you consume
- ✓ Limit alcohol to 1-2 drinks per day

You'll find a link to the complete article in the "Resources" section at the end of this guide.

Killer Mistake #7: Not Getting Enough Sleep

Going through a divorce makes it incredibly difficult to sleep. Your mind is constantly racing with all kinds of thoughts---usually bad. The problem is it is very difficult to turn your mind off once it is engaged. So you end up tossing and turning and sleep deprived.

One of the best things I did when I first separated from my second wife was to call my doctor. I told the nurse about my sleeplessness and she prescribed something to help me gently fall asleep.

It was a true God-send. Once I started sleeping through the night, I discovered new-found strength and energy.

Believe me, it's something we all need, particularly if you're involved in a nasty divorce. This is what mine had become due to my ex- trying to take everything from me.

Without sleep, you will not be mentally sharp when you talk with your attorney. And you won't be emotionally stable when you perform your job.

Unfortunately, a lot of men just say to themselves that insomnia is just part of the process and accept walking around and acting like a zombie. But it doesn't have to be that way.

The combination of getting daily exercise and a nighttime sleep aid works wonders. And you will thank yourself for making such a good investment in yourself.

After a few months, you might even find yourself not needing anything other than a good workout to help you get a good night's sleep.

Killer Mistake #8: Not Keeping "It" In Your Pants

Okay, I'll be the first to admit it. Not having sex for awhile is anything but a pleasant thought. This is particularly true for recently separated men. All we want to do is go out and make a conquest.

It's natural and it is genetic. (At least that's what I told myself.)

But here's the problem with becoming sexually involved so soon after a separation and in the process of a divorce.

You haven't had time to "heal" from your broken marriage. Your self-esteem might be in the tank. You're most likely incredibly needy (wanting sex, sex and more sex.) And regardless of what you tell yourself, you are really not emotionally stable.

So here's some simple advice.

Don't get involved with any women while you're going through your divorce. After all, would you really see any promise in a relationship if the roles were reversed. In other words, what if a needy, emotionally fragile, controlling woman came on to you while out one night.

Would you see any future in that? I don't think you would.

The problem is, if you get into another relationship too quickly, you just postpone the healing and pain everyone must go through in a divorce, IF they want to be a healthy, evolved individual.

And let me be quite honest with you. I've made that mistake after my first marriage. You're thinking nothing like a hot incredible sexual relationship to take your mind off all the gut-wrenching pain of divorce, right?

Wrong.

It took me another 1 ½ years to heal as a result of getting involved so fast. You want to get reacquainted with your self-identity—the one you most likely lost in your marriage.

So here's an idea: take time to reconnect with friends you haven't seen for awhile during your divorce. Go places where you never went because your ex didn't like them. Visit relatives. Get involved in groups that have similar interests, whether they are hobby, vocational or spiritually related.

It really doesn't matter. You will find yourself starting to remember who you are, what you stand for and why you're an incredible individual, without having sex to validate all that.

Killer Mistake #9: Not Being By Yourself Enough

This tip probably has you thinking, "yeah right." After all, who really wants to be alone when you're suffering intense emotional, mental and physical pain. You need to be comforted right?

But I've got news for you. That might work well when you're married but not when you're single. You need to experience your new-found status as a single male.

And much of that time is going to be alone. On the plus side, it gives you time to be introspective. Examine your own thoughts. Think about what you want in life, in a relationship.

No one else knows that answer other than you. Here's the great thing about this approach: no one will be challenging you (as my very controlling ex-wife did). Your answers will always be best and final.

Trust me. It's difficult to get adjusted to. But I found that after 4-5 months, I really started feeling better about my life and myself.

I started thinking about what I wanted to do; not what my wife or children were interested in.

Being selfish is not such a bad thing. Because if you're not true to yourself, who are you going to be true to?

So please. Take the time to enjoy your own company. And if you really need companionship, here's a simple solution: get a dog…or cat…or parakeet or gold fish. Outside of yourself, they'll give you the unconditional love you are so worthy of.

Summary

Suddenly becoming a single male can be a traumatic experience at first. Your world's been turned upside down. You've been betrayed or cast aside by a woman you promised to "love and honor in good times and bad."

But guess what: you're not alone. In fact, in calendar year 2008 more than 1,000,000 men got divorced in the U.S.

My viewpoint is that people don't take their vows seriously anymore. Too much "me generation" has a lot of women (and men) thinking that this person I chose to marry is not making me happy, so I'm going to cheat, or lie or file for divorce. "Screw it, my happiness is more important than anything!"

I don't profess to have an answer. But I can tell you what worked for me in getting through my divorce.

If you avoid these 9 mistakes talked about in this guide, you stand a better than average chance of coming out of your divorce not only stronger, but happier too.

You need not look any further than me. I'm living proof it can happen.

Resources

Qualified therapists:

> ➤ www.psychcentral.com

Infidelity blog & chat room:

> ➤ http://infidelity-support.ning.com/main/authorization/signUp?

Advice for dads:

> ➤ www.dadsdivorce.om

Health insurance:

> ➤ www.einsurance.com

Net wealth calculator:

> ➤ http://cgi.money.cnn.com/tools/networth/networth.html

Nutrition:

> ➤ http://www.mayoclinic.com/health/healthy-diet/NU00190/NSECTIONGROUP=2